FLUTE • PIANO

SOLO BOOKLET INCLUDED

HAL•LEONARD
WEDDING ESSENTIALS

AUDIO ACCESS INCLUDED

PLAYBACK+
Speed • Pitch • Balance • Loop

WEDDING FLUTE SOLOS

T0057691

To access audio visit:
www.halleonard.com/mylibrary

Enter Code
4388-8675-0726-2883

ISBN 978-1-4234-7690-0

HAL•LEONARD® CORPORATION
7777 W. BLUEMOUND RD. P.O. BOX 13819 MILWAUKEE, WI 53213

CAN YOU FEEL THE LOVE TONIGHT

from Walt Disney Pictures' THE LION KING

Music by ELTON JOHN
Lyrics by TIM RICE

17
p
mp
21
24
mf
mp
mf
mp
25
3
29
f
f

33
mp
mp
37
39
mf
mf
41
Freely
rall.
mp
rall.
mp
45
a tempo
p
molto rit.
a tempo
p
molto rit.

GABRIEL'S OBOE
from the Motion Picture THE MISSION

Words and Music by
ENNIO MORRICONE

8
11
13
mp
14
16

rit.
rit.

GROW OLD WITH ME

Words and Music by
JOHN LENNON

13
17
21
25
cresc.

29
mf
33
3
3
37
41
43
mp
3
mp

45
49
53
57
rit.
rit.
a tempo
rit.

HERE, THERE AND EVERYWHERE

Words and Music by JOHN LENNON
and PAUL McCARTNEY

13
16
19
20
22

25
28
31
1.
2.
34
molto rit.
molto rit.

HIGHLAND CATHEDRAL

By MICHAEL KORB
and ULRICH ROEVER

13
16
19
21
22

25
28
31
34
3

37
39
f
3
40
43
46

48
51
54
57
rit.
rit.

I WILL BE HERE

Words and Music by
STEVEN CURTIS CHAPMAN

HAL•LEONARD WEDDING ESSENTIALS

AUDIO ACCESS INCLUDED

PLAYBACK+
Speed • Pitch • Balance • Loop

WEDDING FLUTE SOLOS

HAL•LEONARD® CORPORATION
7777 W. BLUEMOUND RD. P.O. BOX 13819 MILWAUKEE, WI 53213

HL00842457

CAN YOU FEEL THE LOVE TONIGHT

from Walt Disney Pictures' THE LION KING

Flute

Music by ELTON JOHN
Lyrics by TIM RICE

22
24
mf
mp
25
3
28
f
31
35
2
mp
39
mf
rall.
43
Freely
mp
46
a tempo
p
molto rit.

GABRIEL'S OBOE
from the Motion Picture THE MISSION

Flute

Words and Music by
ENNIO MORRICONE

GROW OLD WITH ME

Words and Music by
JOHN LENNON

Flute

HERE, THERE AND EVERYWHERE

Words and Music by JOHN LENNON
and PAUL McCARTNEY

HIGHLAND CATHEDRAL

Flute

By MICHAEL KORB
and ULRICH ROEVER

I WILL BE HERE

Flute

Words and Music by
STEVEN CURTIS CHAPMAN

32
To Coda
36
D.S. al Coda
CODA
39
40
44
3
5
52
56
59
63
67
rit.
p

THE LORD'S PRAYER

Flute

By ALBERT H. MALOTTE

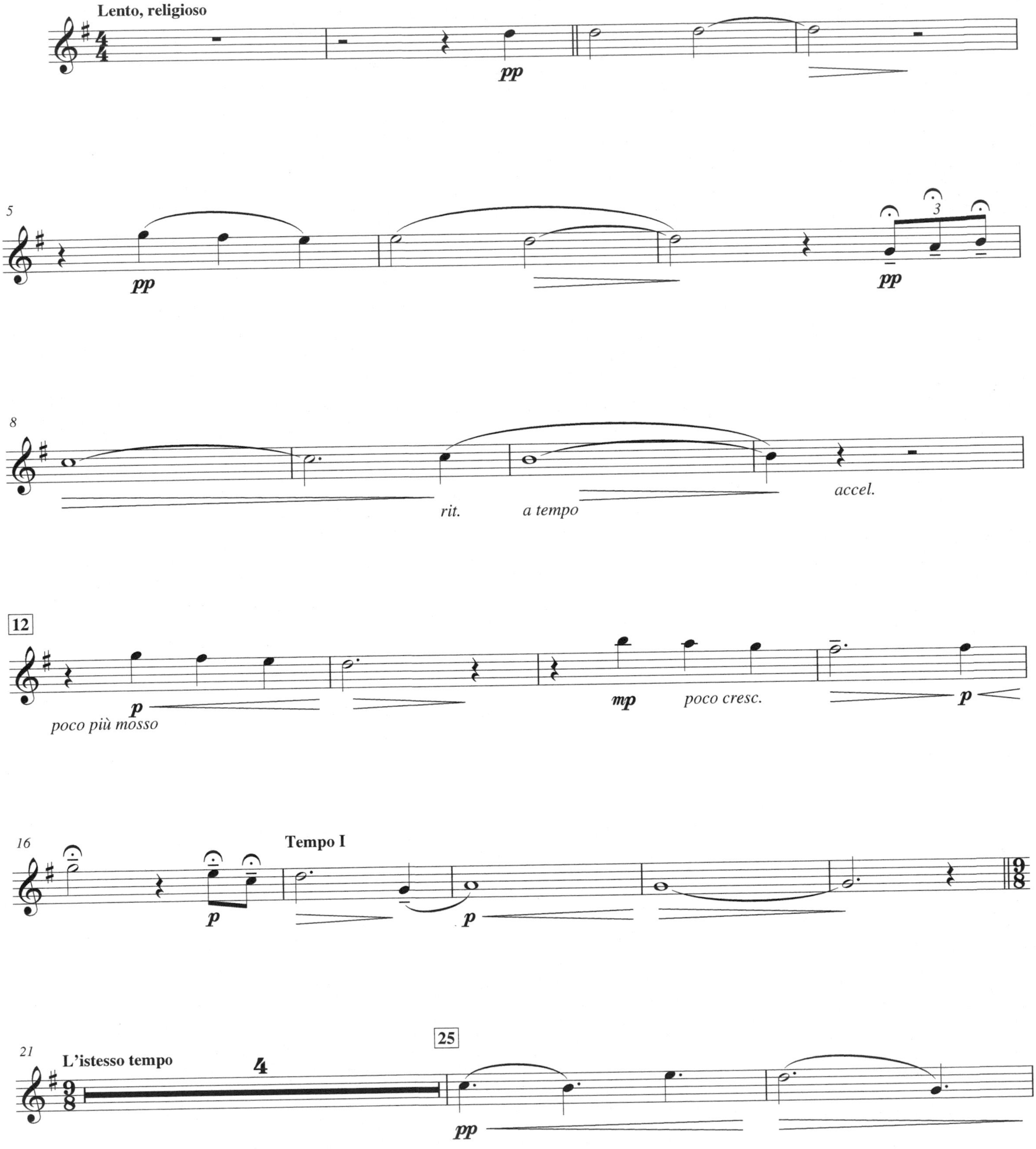

27
p
p
poco accel.
p
31
rallentando
a tempo
34
35
p
37
Poco meno mosso, e sonoramente
mf
mf
rit.
f
40
12/8
ff
43
Tempo I
f
9/8
mf
46
p
rallentando e morendo

SUNRISE, SUNSET

from the Musical FIDDLER ON THE ROOF

Flute

Words by SHELDON HARNICK
Music by JERRY BOCK

47
53
59
65
D.S. al Coda
CODA
a tempo
71
77
83
85
mp
89
95
rit.

WEDDING PROCESSIONAL

from THE SOUND OF MUSIC

Flute

Lyrics by OSCAR HAMMERSTEIN II
Music by RICHARD RODGERS

YOU RAISE ME UP

Flute

Words and Music by BRENDAN GRAHAM
and ROLF LOVLAND

15
19
21
mf
mf
23
26

30
To Coda
34
D.S. al Coda
mp
CODA
39
41

44
3
48
52
55

58
61
64
68
mp
rit.
rit.
p

WEDDING PROCESSIONAL

from THE SOUND OF MUSIC

Lyrics by OSCAR HAMMERSTEIN II
Music by RICHARD RODGERS

13
16
To Coda
19
22

25
For the entrance of the Bride
ff
8vb
28
D.S. al Coda
CODA
31
34
rit.
rit.
8va
8vb

THE LORD'S PRAYER

By ALBERT H. MALOTTE

11
12
accel.
poco più mosso
accel.
14
mp
poco cresc.
Tempo I
18
21
L'istesso tempo
pp molto espressivo e sempre legato

25
pp
p
pp
p
28
p
poco accel.
p
poco accel.
p
Ped.
31
rallentando
a tempo
rallentando
a tempo
pp
p
Ped.
Ped.
34
35
p
p
mp
mp
Ped.

37
Poco meno mosso, e sonoramente
mf
rit.
f
40
ff
43
Tempo I
mf
46
p
rallentando e morendo
pp
ppp
Ped.

SUNRISE, SUNSET

from the Musical FIDDLER ON THE ROOF

Words by SHELDON HARNICK
Music by JERRY BOCK

17
21
25
29

33
To Coda
molto rit.
molto rit.
37
a tempo
a tempo
41
45

49
53
54
59
64
D.S. al Coda

CODA
a tempo
a tempo
73
77
81

85
mp
89
93
97
rit.
rit.

YOU RAISE ME UP

Words and Music by BRENDAN GRAHAM
and ROLF LOVLAND

13
mp
mp
16
19
mf
3
22
mf
23

25
28
1.
f
f
31
2.
dim.
dim.
mp freely
33
mp freely
34